JACOB (BIBLICAL CHARACTERS SERIES)

JACOB (BIBLICAL CHARACTERS SERIES)

JAMES WHITELAW

Swackie Ltd

CONTENTS

Introduction		1
1	Jacob's Birth	2
2	Buying a Birthright	5
3	Stealing a blessing	7
4	Making an Enemy	11
5	Fleeing for Life	15
6	Jacob's Ladder at Bethel	17
7	Rachel, Love at First Sight	20
8	The Deceiver Meets his Match	23
9	Jacob's Children	27
10	The Battle of the Deceivers	31
11	Jacob Flees Again	35
12	Treaty with Laban	39
13	Jacob Bargains with God	44
14	The Deceiver Turns Winner	48

15	Jacob and Esau Reconcile	51
16	Dinah's Shame Revenged	54
17	Return to Bethel	58
18	Death of Rachel	61
19	Joseph Lost	63
20	Joseph Found	67
21	Down to Egypt	70
22	Jacob's Death	73
Author's Note		76

Introduction

The story of Jacob gives me hope. Jacob is no less than a rogue. If Jacob were alive in the twenty-first century, he would be one of those ruthless entrepreneurs who would take advantage of their staff and pay them a pittance. He would outwit his competitors and pull every trick in the book. Jacob would be the JR Ewing.

Jacob is well named as his name means 'Deceiver'. There is no depth he will not stoop to in his efforts to get ahead. He manipulates his entire family and then runs off when it gets too hot to stick around.

Despite this less than desirable character, God has chosen Jacob, and throughout his life, God overlooks Jacob's weaknesses while he works on his character to make him a better person.

Why does Jacob give me hope? Quite simply, if God can love, choose and accept a character like Jacob, then he will accept me, who has failed him continually for the past sixty years.

The story of Jacob is the story of God's sovereignty and of God's faithfulness towards those he chooses. It is also the story of God's abundant blessings poured out on his people and even those associated with them.

As we read the story of this lying, cheating, manipulating rogue, we will see God working out his plans, regardless of what any man plans.

Jacob is the last of the patriarchs, and he fathers the twelve tribes of Israel who will be the defining leaders and division of the nation.

As we work our way through this study, let us consider the weaknesses of Jacob and although it all worked out in the end, note that Jacob, at the end of his life, said his "days had been few and unpleasant".

God can still work out his plans despite us, can still use us for his purposes, but if we fight against him, it will be unpleasant for us also.

CHAPTER 1

Jacob's Birth

Genesis 25:19-28

This is the account of the family line of Abraham's son Isaac.

Abraham became the father of Isaac, and Isaac was forty years old when he married Rebekah daughter of Bethuel the Aramean from Paddan Aram and sister of Laban the Aramean.

Isaac prayed to the Lord on behalf of his wife, because she was childless. The Lord answered his prayer, and his wife Rebekah became pregnant. The babies jostled each other within her, and she said, "Why is this happening to me?" So she went to inquire of the Lord.

The Lord said to her,

"Two nations are in your womb, and two peoples from within you will be separated; one people will be stronger than the other, and the older will serve the younger."

When the time came for her to give birth, there were twin boys in her womb. The first to come out was red, and his whole body was like a hairy garment; so they named him Esau. After this, his brother came out, with his hand grasping Esau's heel; so he was named Jacob. Isaac was sixty years old when Rebekah gave birth to them.

The boys grew up, and Esau became a skillful hunter, a man of the open country, while Jacob was content to stay at home among the tents. Isaac, who had a taste for wild game, loved Esau, but Rebekah loved Jacob.

Jacob was born into a dysfunctional family where his father was weak and easily manipulated, and his mother took advantage of that. He was a twin, and they were destined to be enemies before they were even born.

Jacob was the younger of the two twins, but God had told Rebekah that the younger brother would be the dominant one and the older brother would serve him.

As the two brothers grew up, they were used as pawns on a chessboard by two parents who favoured different boys. The two boys were distinct in almost every way. While Esau was red, hairy and rough, Jacob would have been almost feminine.

Esau took life in his stride and just accepted what came his way without giving it very much thought, but Jacob calculated everything out before acting.

Esau was an outdoorsman and a very skillful hunter, we are told, while Jacob preferred to stay indoors and was said to be peaceful. Despite his indoor life, however, at some point, he did manage to become a skilled shepherd.

Every one of us is born into a dysfunctional world, and we face trouble all our lives, but just like Jacob and Esau, we are known to God before we are born. God knows what we will be like and how we will turn out. The very fact that you are reading this book tells me that God favours you.

God had mapped out your life before you were born, and he has called you to be his child and carry out the work that he has determined for you.

None of us is precisely the same, and none of us has the same task to complete.

However, the trials we come up against and the problems we will face are all the same, and we can learn by studying these characters from four thousand years ago. In this study, we will examine the life of Jacob and learn from the many mistakes he makes.

Does this mean we will not make mistakes? Absolutely not. We will make mistakes and perhaps even the same ones Jacob made, but we have the comfort that God will look after us in the same way he looked after Jacob. We also have the assurance that God will work out his plans despite any interference from any other person or group, including ourselves.

As each of us will be different and carry out various tasks in the Kingdom, we must accept that others are different and do not try to make others like us. There is only one of us, and we are unique.

CHAPTER 2

Buying a Birthright

Genesis 25:29-34
Once when Jacob was cooking some stew, Esau came in from the open country, famished. He said to Jacob, "Quick, let me have some of that red stew! I'm famished!" (That is why he was also called Edom.)
Jacob replied, "First sell me your birthright."
Look, I am about to die," Esau said. "What good is the birthright to me?"
But Jacob said, "Swear to me first." So he swore an oath to him, selling his birthright to Jacob.
Then Jacob gave Esau some bread and some lentil stew. He ate and drank, and then got up and left.
So Esau despised his birthright.

The ruthless entrepreneur in Jacob was waiting on the right opportunity. He knew what he wanted and would have been waiting and watching for the right moment to obtain what he desired.

This opportunity came out of the blue one day when Esau returned from hunting, extremely hungry and looking for something to eat. Jacob refused to give him some of the stew he was cooking until Esau gave him his birthright as payment.

Esau swore to Jacob to give him his birthright, and then Jacob gave him some stew. The birthright meant little to Esau, who ate his meal and went on his way without thinking about it much.

This was all part of God's plan, but that does not excuse Jacob from being unreasonable and manipulative. If you have started down the Christian road, this sort of behaviour is unacceptable to God, and you may not get off with it as easily as Jacob did. Others, throughout the Bible, have faced severe punishment for a lot less.

Under the law of Christ, we are to prefer others to ourselves, so we should not model ourselves on Jacob's behaviour. On the other hand, neither should we be like Esau and allow ourselves to be walked all over.

Part of the problem here is the attitude of the brothers. While Jacob was manipulating and taking advantage of his brother, Esau is careless with what God had given him. Of course, we should not take advantage of another person, but neither should we act with contempt in safeguarding what God has given us.

The case for sovereign choice and that God chooses some and not others can be complex for some Christians to accept. On the one hand, we are given free will to decide whether to accept Jesus as saviour, but then we are also chosen from before the foundation of the earth.

God is sovereign, and we must accept that. How this fits around our free will and choice to accept Jesus is a mystery that we will see clearly when we finally go home to heaven. Until then, we simply need to acknowledge that God chose us and praise him for this.

CHAPTER 3

Stealing a blessing

Genesis 27:1-29

When Isaac was old and his eyes were so weak that he could no longer see, he called for Esau his older son and said to him, "My son."

"Here I am," he answered.

Isaac said, "I am now an old man and don't know the day of my death. Now then, get your equipment—your quiver and bow—and go out to the open country to hunt some wild game for me. Prepare me the kind of tasty food I like and bring it to me to eat, so that I may give you my blessing before I die."

Now Rebekah was listening as Isaac spoke to his son Esau. When Esau left for the open country to hunt game and bring it back, Rebekah said to her son Jacob, "Look, I overheard your father say to your brother Esau, 'Bring me some game and prepare me some tasty food to eat, so that I may give you my blessing in the presence of the Lord before I die.' Now, my son, listen carefully and do what I tell you: Go out to the flock and bring me two choice young goats, so I can prepare some tasty food for your father, just the way he likes it. Then take it to your father to eat, so that he may give you his blessing before he dies."

Jacob said to Rebekah his mother, "But my brother Esau is a hairy man while I have smooth skin. What if my father touches me? I would appear to be tricking him and would bring down a curse on myself rather than a blessing."

His mother said to him, "My son, let the curse fall on me. Just do what I say; go and get them for me."

So he went and got them and brought them to his mother, and she prepared some tasty food, just the way his father liked it. Then Rebekah took the best clothes of Esau her older son, which she had in the house, and put them on her younger son Jacob. She also covered his hands and the smooth part of his neck with the goatskins. Then she handed to her son Jacob the tasty food and the bread she had made.

He went to his father and said, "My father."

"Yes, my son," he answered. "Who is it?"

Jacob said to his father, "I am Esau your firstborn. I have done as you told me. Please sit up and eat some of my game, so that you may give me your blessing."

Isaac asked his son, "How did you find it so quickly, my son?"

"The Lord your God gave me success," he replied.

Then Isaac said to Jacob, "Come near so I can touch you, my son, to know whether you really are my son Esau or not."

Jacob went close to his father Isaac, who touched him and said, "The voice is the voice of Jacob, but the hands are the hands of Esau." He did not recognize him, for his hands were hairy like those of his brother Esau; so he proceeded to bless him. "Are you really my son Esau?" he asked.

"I am," he replied.

Then he said, "My son, bring me some of your game to eat, so that I may give you my blessing."

Jacob brought it to him and he ate; and he brought some wine and he drank. Then his father Isaac said to him, "Come here, my son, and kiss me."

So he went to him and kissed him. When Isaac caught the smell of his clothes, he blessed him and said,

"Ah, the smell of my son is like the smell of a field that the Lord has blessed. May God give you heaven's dew and earth's richness—an abundance of grain and new wine.

May nations serve you and peoples bow down to you. Be lord over your brothers, and may the sons of your mother bow down to you. May those who curse you be cursed and those who bless you be blessed."

Jacob wasn't happy just with Esau's birthright but wanted the chief blessing from his father too. This wasn't so easy to effect, but Jacob and his mother cobbled together an elaborate plan to deceive Issac into giving Jacob the blessing.

Not only was this extremely deceitful, but it was also very disrespectful to his father. Rebekah would surely have told Jacob about the prophecy given to her before the birth of the twins, but it shows the complete lack of faith on the part of both of them that they had to take matters into their own hands to ensure that it actually happened.

Jacob is very wary and doesn't think they will manage to carry the plan out, but Rebekah reassures him and comes up with a solution to every problem they face to ensure the success of their deception. It is important to note that Rebekah is willing to shoulder the blame if they are caught out. She is most likely confident that she can manipulate her husband if this happens. However, she cannot manipulate God, and beyond this episode, we never hear of Rebekah again.

Isaac here is very old, weak and can barely see. He can be likened to the Church in our day, weak and powerless, scarcely able to distinguish between right and wrong. The world is easily able to manipulate the Church today, just as Rebekah manipulated Isaac.

Isaac was suspicious as he recognised Jacob's voice. A stronger father would have thought it through and prevented the injustice from happening, but Isaac was well used to being passive and walked over.

Isaac delivers the blessing, which should have gone to Esau, which gave Jacob the best of everything on the earth, including the rule over his brother and other nations.

The old family trait of taking shortcuts is in play here, and neither Jacob nor Rebekah are prepared to wait for God to carry out his plans in his own time. Instead, they are once again taking matters into their own hands. This seems to be something which happens in every generation of this family, but if we study our own history, we also are prone to this mistake. It is one of the biggest problems in Christian life.

Over and over again, in this study of Jacob's life, the message will be that God is sovereign and works out his sovereign plans regardless of man's plans. So in a sense, it doesn't matter what we do. God's plans will prevail. However, it would be folly to be complacent, as this shows the same disrespect to Almighty God that Jacob showed to his father.

This deception carried out by Rebekah and Jacob is of the worst we could imagine happening within any family, let alone the family God has chosen to bless the entire world through. This family is out of step with God, just as the Church is mainly out of step with God today.

Despite this, God's hand is still on this family, moulding it and shaping it to his design and accomplishing what he has determined. He will do the same with his Church and restore it to reflect his glory when the time is right.

CHAPTER 4

Making an Enemy

Genesis 27:30-46

After Isaac finished blessing him, and Jacob had scarcely left his father's presence, his brother Esau came in from hunting. He too prepared some tasty food and brought it to his father. Then he said to him, "My father, please sit up and eat some of my game, so that you may give me your blessing."

His father Isaac asked him, "Who are you?"

"I am your son," he answered, "your firstborn, Esau."

Isaac trembled violently and said, "Who was it, then, that hunted game and brought it to me? I ate it just before you came and I blessed him—and indeed he will be blessed!"

When Esau heard his father's words, he burst out with a loud and bitter cry and said to his father, "Bless me—me too, my father!"

But he said, "Your brother came deceitfully and took your blessing."

Esau said, "Isn't he rightly named Jacob? This is the second time he has taken advantage of me: He took my birthright, and now he's taken my blessing!" Then he asked, "Haven't you reserved any blessing for me?"

Isaac answered Esau, "I have made him lord over you and have made all his relatives his servants, and I have sustained him with grain and new wine. So what can I possibly do for you, my son?"

Esau said to his father, "Do you have only one blessing, my father? Bless me too, my father!" Then Esau wept aloud.

His father Isaac answered him, "Your dwelling will be away from the earth's richness, away from the dew of heaven above. You will live by the sword and you will serve your brother. But when you grow restless, you will throw his yoke from off your neck."

Esau held a grudge against Jacob because of the blessing his father had given him. He said to himself, "The days of mourning for my father are near; then I will kill my brother Jacob."

When Rebekah was told what her older son Esau had said, she sent for her younger son Jacob and said to him, "Your brother Esau is planning to avenge himself by killing you. Now then, my son, do what I say: Flee at once to my brother Laban in Harran. Stay with him for a while until your brother's fury subsides. When your brother is no longer angry with you and forgets what you did to him, I'll send word for you to come back from there. Why should I lose both of you in one day?"

Then Rebekah said to Isaac, "I'm disgusted with living because of these Hittite women. If Jacob takes a wife from among the women of this land, from Hittite women like these, my life will not be worth living."

Oh, dear! What a state this family is now in. Outright war is declared, and who could blame Esau. Of course, he was well aware that Jacob had tricked him and took advantage of obtaining his birthright, but this was the last straw that broke the camel's back.

Esau is bitterly disappointed and angry at this turn of events. Perhaps Esau did not care too much about the birthright as he knew the blessing would make him superior, but that also was whipped away from him in a cruel manner.

Esau had every right to be angry, and when we read other places in scripture, we see men being killed for much less. In truth, Jacob deserved to die for this deception, and Esau intended to make sure it happened.

It is ironic, though, that where Jacob lacked respect for his father, Esau, the black sheep, still retains enough respect that he will not kill Jacob while his father is alive.

Rebekah sees the danger for Jacob and again starts to weave her web to construct the outcome she wants. She starts to convince Isaac that Jacob needs to leave. Notably, she conveys to Jacob that she wants him to flee to her brother, Laban, but does not say that to Isaac. Yet, Isaac comes to the same conclusion. A master manipulator at work.

The big cry in life these days is to look after number one. I guess Jacob would claim this is what he is doing, and he certainly does not seem to bother about who gets hurt. But, unfortunately, it is not the way of God and taking this attitude will result in us suffering somehow.

Sometimes we will look at those who continually abuse their position and advantage and ask the question, 'How are they allowed to get away with it?' Something like this must have been going through Esau's head, and he must be starting to think that God is not fair.

This is something that we will hear in our Christian walk, and we cannot refute it. God is sovereign, and he favours who he favours, and none can demand why of him. I could ask, 'why was I born into a Christian country and a Christian family, while others are brought into the world in poverty and adversity?'

We, as Christians, will have to listen to accounts of how other Christians have taken advantage and abused non-believers and believers alike. We will have no answer, but let us strive to reflect the goodness and love of God all around.

Jacob is intent on his own success, but we as Christians must prefer others before ourselves. We must be seeking first the Kingdom of God. If we act in the same manner as Jacob, we may well secure our own fortune in this world, but we will never advance the Kingdom of our father and never convince any lost sinner that we have something for which is worth striving.

If we act in the manner Jacob and Rebekah did, then we send a message to the world that we are no different from them. Indeed they will be convinced that Christians are the worst of all sorts.

CHAPTER 5

Fleeing for Life

Genesis 28:1-5
So Isaac called for Jacob and blessed him. Then he commanded him: "Do not marry a Canaanite woman. Go at once to Paddan Aram, to the house of your mother's father Bethuel. Take a wife for yourself there, from among the daughters of Laban, your mother's brother. May God Almighty bless you and make you fruitful and increase your numbers until you become a community of peoples. May he give you and your descendants the blessing given to Abraham, so that you may take possession of the land where you now reside as a foreigner, the land God gave to Abraham." Then Isaac sent Jacob on his way, and he went to Paddan Aram, to Laban son of Bethuel the Aramean, the brother of Rebekah, who was the mother of Jacob and Esau.

It all sounds so civilised in this passage, but behind the scenes, Rebekah is manipulating her husband into a corner, and Jacob is fleeing from a brother he has made so angry, he wants to kill him.

Isaac blesses Jacob again, showing that he is pretty much just doing as he is told. Isaac has always been keen on an easy life, and I guess it was easiest to send Jacob away, as it would be one less problem with which to deal.

Isaac had enough problems already with Esau. Moreover, although Isaac favoured Esau, problems were primarily related to his unbelieving wives, so Rebekah would have found it reasonably easy to play on those concerns.

Jacob's scheming has caught up on him, and he is forced to flee for his life, but ironically, he goes with Isaac's blessing. This, incidentally, will be the last time Jacob will see his mother, as she will have died before he returns twenty years later, her death not even being recorded for us.

Although all this is working out and looks like chaos resulting from problems and bitterness, it is all within God's plan, and Jacob is heading for a different encounter and a change in circumstances.

If we live our lives in the same manner as Jacob, then we will end up in the same position. We will end up fleeing from our problems, only to encounter other issues.

We will also send a message to the watching world that Christianity is not worth considering. All this talk of praying to God to answer all your needs doesn't work, or why would Christians resort to these dishonest ways of gain?

CHAPTER 6

Jacob's Ladder at Bethel

Genesis 28:10-22

Jacob left Beersheba and set out for Harran. When he reached a certain place, he stopped for the night because the sun had set. Taking one of the stones there, he put it under his head and lay down to sleep. He had a dream in which he saw a stairway resting on the earth, with its top reaching to heaven, and the angels of God were ascending and descending on it. There above it stood the Lord, and he said: "I am the Lord, the God of your father Abraham and the God of Isaac. I will give you and your descendants the land on which you are lying. Your descendants will be like the dust of the earth, and you will spread out to the west and to the east, to the north and to the south. All peoples on earth will be blessed through you and your offspring. I am with you and will watch over you wherever you go, and I will bring you back to this land. I will not leave you until I have done what I have promised you."

When Jacob awoke from his sleep, he thought, "Surely the Lord is in this place, and I was not aware of it." He was afraid and said, "How awesome is this place! This is none other than the house of God; this is the gate of heaven."

Early the next morning Jacob took the stone he had placed under his head and set it up as a pillar and poured oil on top of it. He called that place Bethel, though the city used to be called Luz.

Then Jacob made a vow, saying, "If God will be with me and will watch over me on this journey I am taking and will give me food to eat and clothes to wear so that I return safely to my father's household, then the Lord will be my God and this stone that I have set up as a pillar will be God's house, and of all that you give me I will give you a tenth."

By this time, most of us would have written Jacob off as a bad egg, not worth wasting our time and efforts on him. But, it just goes to show, our ways are not the same as God's ways. Jacob had only gone a short distance when God appeared to him.

God chooses this time to make himself known to Jacob and renew the promises he had made to his father and grandfather. Thus, God confirms, not only will Jacob be blessed, but all the families of the earth will be blessed through him.

God's promise to Jacob is thorough, pledging to be with him until he returns to the land he is leaving. God reaffirms the covenant with Jacob and again promises that his descendants will be like the dust of the earth.

What is Jacob's response? Jacob is delighted, but he is still not wholly bought over to God's cause, as he still tries to make a bargain with God. Here is God promising Jacob, literally the entire world, and Jacob still tries to set conditions.

It is so unfair. After all Jacob has done, here he is being rewarded beyond even his own wildest dreams. This is a sovereign God in action, working out his plans, not just for Jacob but also for the entire world. God has a much bigger plan in play, and Jacob is merely one of those characters involved.

God is not restricted by ordinary rules or by everyday events. He is not even limited to using good men. Indeed, very often, God takes bad men and makes them good, which he sets out to do with Jacob.

We will see the same in our times. As we look around, we see the testimony of many men or women who once rebelled and fought against God but was turned in an instant, or perhaps over a more extended period.

God is also doing this in your life. You may well think perhaps that you are not a bad person as you measure yourself against other men. However, read more about Jesus and measure yourself against him, and I am sure you will come to the same conclusion I have.

I am like black against the white of Jesus. Where Jesus continually thought of others, my thinking is always tinged with a little 'What is in it for me?' The truth is, the more we get to know Jesus, the more we realise just how poor and pathetic we are ourselves.

Against this realisation, we begin to accept that the only way we have anything worth within us is what God gives us. Indeed, we realise that every good thing that has happened to us in life has been at God's instruction, and it is a humbling discovery.

From this point, we further discover that our real strength lies not within ourselves but in the indwelling of Jesus within us. This dawning liberates power undreamed within us and allows us to accomplish great things.

Jacob is not quite there yet, though. He certainly gets an eye-opener at Bethel but fails to grasp the whole truth of what God is doing in his life. That acceptance will take another twenty years.

CHAPTER 7

Rachel, Love at First Sight

<u>Rachel, Love at First Sight</u>
<u>Genesis 29:1-14</u>

Then Jacob continued on his journey and came to the land of the eastern peoples. There he saw a well in the open country, with three flocks of sheep lying near it because the flocks were watered from that well. The stone over the mouth of the well was large. When all the flocks were gathered there, the shepherds would roll the stone away from the well's mouth and water the sheep. Then they would return the stone to its place over the mouth of the well.

Jacob asked the shepherds, "My brothers, where are you from?"

"We're from Harran," they replied.

He said to them, "Do you know Laban, Nahor's grandson?"

"Yes, we know him," they answered.

Then Jacob asked them, "Is he well?"

"Yes, he is," they said, "and here comes his daughter Rachel with the sheep."

"Look," he said, "the sun is still high; it is not time for the flocks to be gathered. Water the sheep and take them back to pasture."

"We can't," they replied, *"until all the flocks are gathered and the stone has been rolled away from the mouth of the well. Then we will water the sheep."*

While he was still talking with them, Rachel came with her father's sheep, for she was a shepherd. When Jacob saw Rachel daughter of his uncle Laban, and Laban's sheep, he went over and rolled the stone away from the mouth of the well and watered his uncle's sheep. Then Jacob kissed Rachel and began to weep aloud. He had told Rachel that he was a relative of her father and a son of Rebekah. So she ran and told her father.

As soon as Laban heard the news about Jacob, his sister's son, he hurried to meet him. He embraced him and kissed him and brought him to his home, and there Jacob told him all these things. Then Laban said to him, "You are my own flesh and blood."

Jacob finally arrives in Haran and seeks out his uncle. Firstly, he is very fortunate to meet with his cousin, Rachel, and he immediately falls head over heels for her.

Rachel excitedly runs to tell her father, and Jacob is welcomed into the family home. Jacob relates his story to Laban, although I am sure it would have been different from what Esau would have told.

It seems to us to be a fortunate encounter, but in fact, this was all carefully planned by God. Everything in Jacob's life until this point has led him up to this place where his life would change. For the first time in Jacob's life, Jacob sees something else worthy of his attention, apart from himself.

Reading from this point forward, we will see a marked change in Jacob's behaviour, and he is no longer so rash and thoughtless. Instead, Jacob's sights are now set on the love of his life, and he is diligently patient in pursuing that love.

So it is with Christians when we find Jesus. We are overwhelmed by his beauty, kindness, compassion, and unconditional love for us that we are changed forever. From that point forward, we are committed to our pursuit of Godliness and to be more like him.

Jacob is still acting the bravado at this point, as he ignores the other shepherds, ignores the local custom and goes straight to the well and rolls the stone away. This bravado will soon be beaten out of him by someone who is his match.

CHAPTER 8

The Deceiver Meets his Match

<u>The Deceiver Meets his Match</u>
Genesis 29:14-30

After Jacob had stayed with him for a whole month, Laban said to him, "Just because you are a relative of mine, should you work for me for nothing? Tell me what your wages should be."

Now Laban had two daughters; the name of the older was Leah, and the name of the younger was Rachel. Leah had weak eyes, but Rachel had a lovely figure and was beautiful. Jacob was in love with Rachel and said, "I'll work for you seven years in return for your younger daughter Rachel."

Laban said, "It's better that I give her to you than to some other man. Stay here with me." So Jacob served seven years to get Rachel, but they seemed like only a few days to him because of his love for her.

Then Jacob said to Laban, "Give me my wife. My time is completed, and I want to make love to her."

So Laban brought together all the people of the place and gave a feast. But when evening came, he took his daughter Leah and brought her to Jacob, and Jacob made love to her. And Laban gave his servant Zilpah to his daughter as her attendant.

When morning came, there was Leah! So Jacob said to Laban, "What is this you have done to me? I served you for Rachel, didn't I? Why have you deceived me?"

Laban replied, "It is not our custom here to give the younger daughter in marriage before the older one. Finish this daughter's bridal week; then we will give you the younger one also, in return for another seven years of work."

And Jacob did so. He finished the week with Leah, and then Laban gave him his daughter Rachel to be his wife. Laban gave his servant Bilhah to his daughter Rachel as her attendant. Jacob made love to Rachel also, and his love for Rachel was greater than his love for Leah. And he worked for Laban another seven years.

Jacob meets his match here, and it is easy to see that Rebekah and Laban are from the same family and have passed the common traits down to Jacob.

After Jacob has been there for one month, Laban may be concerned that he is not pulling his weight and wants to tie him down to work for him. He may also have already noticed that God was with Jacob, and he was being blessed as a result. Negotiations begin, and Laban is probably delighted to have got such a bargain.

Jacob agrees to work seven years in return for Rachel's hand in marriage. He works the entire seven years, and because of his love for Rachel, we are told that those seven years seemed like only days.

When the seven years are up, Jacob meets his match in Laban as he is tricked into marrying the wrong sister and has to work a further seven years for Rachel's hand. This is a bizarre tale indeed, and we wonder how is it possible that Jacob, having loved Rachel for seven years, could make this mistake.

I am not sure what the answer to that questions is, but there are various possibilities. First, we must remember that these happenings were passed on by word of mouth and were only committed to writing some four hundred years later by Moses so that the events could have been jumbled up a bit by this time.

It may also have been at the feast which Laban laid on, there was much strong drink, and Jacob had too much of it. If it was, then it cost him dearly.

We have to accept that the deception that took place was successful, and we will never know exactly how it happened. The same explanation will apply when we come to look at the timing of the birth of Jacob's first twelve children, who all arrived over seven years.

Here, Jacob meets his match. Just as Jacob took advantage of Esau, it is now payback time, and Jacob, in turn, is tricked by a master. Jacob now knows what Esau felt like, and it may now be dawning on him the trouble he caused.

Even if we are Christians, we are not absolved from trouble, and indeed, we can expect it if we continue to mistreat people. God may well favour us, but this does not mean that we will not pay the price for our wrongdoings. We may even pay a higher cost than non-believers, as much more is expected of us who know what is right and wrong.

There may also be a message for us in this passage regarding waiting for God's time and passing the waiting time working and showing a good example.

We can assume that God has all this planned, and he is using this time to take Jacob down a peg or two and teach him some lessons. There is very little told about what happened during the twenty years with Laban, but there is no doubt the Jacob travelling south after twenty years is not the same Jacob who had just arrived in Haran.

CHAPTER 9

Jacob's Children

Genesis 29:31-35 & 30:1-24

When the Lord saw that Leah was not loved, he enabled her to conceive, but Rachel remained childless. Leah became pregnant and gave birth to a son. She named him Reuben, for she said, "It is because the Lord has seen my misery. Surely my husband will love me now."

She conceived again, and when she gave birth to a son she said, "Because the Lord heard that I am not loved, he gave me this one too." So she named him Simeon.

Again she conceived, and when she gave birth to a son she said, "Now at last my husband will become attached to me, because I have borne him three sons." So he was named Levi.

She conceived again, and when she gave birth to a son she said, "This time I will praise the Lord." So she named him Judah. Then she stopped having children.

When Rachel saw that she was not bearing Jacob any children, she became jealous of her sister. So she said to Jacob, "Give me children, or I'll die!"

Jacob became angry with her and said, "Am I in the place of God, who has kept you from having children?"

Then she said, "Here is Bilhah, my servant. Sleep with her so that she can bear children for me and I too can build a family through her."

So she gave him her servant Bilhah as a wife. Jacob slept with her, and she became pregnant and bore him a son. Then Rachel said, "God has vindicated me; he has listened to my plea and given me a son." Because of this she named him Dan.

Rachel's servant Bilhah conceived again and bore Jacob a second son. Then Rachel said, "I have had a great struggle with my sister, and I have won." So she named him Naphtali.

When Leah saw that she had stopped having children, she took her servant Zilpah and gave her to Jacob as a wife. Leah's servant Zilpah bore Jacob a son. Then Leah said, "What good fortune!" So she named him Gad.

Leah's servant Zilpah bore Jacob a second son. Then Leah said, "How happy I am! The women will call me happy." So she named him Asher.

During wheat harvest, Reuben went out into the fields and found some mandrake plants, which he brought to his mother Leah. Rachel said to Leah, "Please give me some of your son's mandrakes."

But she said to her, "Wasn't it enough that you took away my husband? Will you take my son's mandrakes too?"

"Very well," Rachel said, "he can sleep with you tonight in return for your son's mandrakes."

So when Jacob came in from the fields that evening, Leah went out to meet him. "You must sleep with me," she said. "I have hired you with my son's mandrakes." So he slept with her that night.

God listened to Leah, and she became pregnant and bore Jacob a fifth son. Then Leah said, "God has rewarded me for giving my servant to my husband." So she named him Issachar.

Leah conceived again and bore Jacob a sixth son. Then Leah said, "God has presented me with a precious gift. This time my husband will treat me with honor, because I have borne him six sons." So she named him Zebulun.

Some time later she gave birth to a daughter and named her Dinah.

> *Then God remembered Rachel; he listened to her and enabled her to conceive. She became pregnant and gave birth to a son and said, "God has taken away my disgrace." She named him Joseph, and said, "May the Lord add to me another son."*

That's quite some passage, both in length and in the content. One thing is sure, Jacob is definitely being fruitful and multiplying. We can now see the beginning of a nation and, with it, the beginning of bickering and jealousies. The competition for their husbands favour with Leah and Rachel is quite something else.

Can any woman reading this book imagine giving her husband to your sister for a few plants? The truth is that is a lot more to the story than told here. Mandrakes are a plant with a root that looks similar to the human body.

Much superstition surrounds mandrakes, and it was probably believed that they made the woman fertile.

Rachel is desperate to have children and believes that these plant will help her conceive. The picture emerging here is that Jacob's relatives had little or no knowledge of the one true God and were steeped in idolatry. Rachel is so desperate that for the sake of a few mandrakes, which perhaps she believes have magical powers, she is willing to give her husband to her sister. It's complicated!!

God is often the great leveller. The story of the two sisters is challenging to comprehend. It was not Jacob's fault that he got landed with two wives. He did not seek out two wives, but this result came about through deceit, similar to what Jacob had planned, back in Canaan.

It was payback time in more ways than one. While Jacob was getting a taste of his own medicine, God also pitied Leah, who Jacob did not love. Leah is very well aware that Jacob did not love her, but what did she expect. Leah must have been party to her father's deceit. She knew Jacob wanted Rachel.

Leah bears Jacob four sons, and Rachel gets jealous. Rachel even goes as far as to attack Jacob and blame him for her not having children. By this time, Jacob is getting stressed out and is easily talked into sleeping with Rachel's maid, Bilhah, who bears him a further two children.

Now Leah is afraid that Rachel is catching up, so she also gives her maid to Jacob, and having done this for Rachel, I guess he could not refuse, so Zilpah gave him another two sons, bringing the total to eight. Leah must have been delighted when she then became pregnant again and, indeed, three times, bearing a further two sons and a daughter to her husband.

Finally, God takes pity on Rachel, and Rachel bears a son, Joseph, to Jacob. This brings the total number of children to eleven sons and one daughter. Benjamin does not come along until later.

The timing of all these events are difficult to piece together, and something seems to have been lost in the telling and re-telling of the story before Moses actually wrote it down.

It is also important to note that unlike in Abraham's case, where the children born to a maid were not included in the promise, here all children are included. I think this difference lies not in the fact that they were born to a maid but rather because Ishamel was born due to unbelief, and this was not the case here.

In the old testament, the call was always to be fruitful and multiply, and this was taken to mean literally and physically. In the new testament, the call is different. The call to us today is to go forth and disciple others. How are we doing on that?

CHAPTER 10

The Battle of the Deceivers

<u>The Battle of the Deceivers</u>
Genesis 30:25-43

After Rachel gave birth to Joseph, Jacob said to Laban, "Send me on my way so I can go back to my own homeland. Give me my wives and children, for whom I have served you, and I will be on my way. You know how much work I've done for you."

But Laban said to him, "If I have found favor in your eyes, please stay. I have learned by divination that the Lord has blessed me because of you." He added, "Name your wages, and I will pay them."

Jacob said to him, "You know how I have worked for you and how your livestock has fared under my care. The little you had before I came has increased greatly, and the Lord has blessed you wherever I have been. But now, when may I do something for my own household?"

"What shall I give you?" he asked.

"Don't give me anything," Jacob replied. "But if you will do this one thing for me, I will go on tending your flocks and watching over them: Let me go through all your flocks today and remove from them every speckled or spotted sheep, every dark-colored lamb and every spotted or speckled goat.

They will be my wages. And my honesty will testify for me in the future, whenever you check on the wages you have paid me. Any goat in my possession that is not speckled or spotted, or any lamb that is not dark-colored, will be considered stolen."

"Agreed," said Laban. "Let it be as you have said." That same day he removed all the male goats that were streaked or spotted, and all the speckled or spotted female goats (all that had white on them) and all the dark-colored lambs, and he placed them in the care of his sons. Then he put a three-day journey between himself and Jacob, while Jacob continued to tend the rest of Laban's flocks.

Jacob, however, took fresh-cut branches from poplar, almond and plane trees and made white stripes on them by peeling the bark and exposing the white inner wood of the branches. Then he placed the peeled branches in all the watering troughs, so that they would be directly in front of the flocks when they came to drink. When the flocks were in heat and came to drink, they mated in front of the branches. And they bore young that were streaked or speckled or spotted. Jacob set apart the young of the flock by themselves, but made the rest face the streaked and dark-colored animals that belonged to Laban. Thus he made separate flocks for himself and did not put them with Laban's animals. Whenever the stronger females were in heat, Jacob would place the branches in the troughs in front of the animals so they would mate near the branches, but if the animals were weak, he would not place them there. So the weak animals went to Laban and the strong ones to Jacob. In this way the man grew exceedingly prosperous and came to own large flocks, and female and male servants, and camels and donkeys.

Uncle and nephew are so alike, and it is difficult to tell who was the trickiest one. I think they would have been evenly matched if God was not with Jacob to prosper him. I am confident the proposal made by Jacob would have seemed to Laban that he was getting the best of the deal, but Jacob was one step ahead of him and was making sure he was coming out on top.

In Chapter 31 v 41, Jacob states that Laban changed his wages ten times during his twenty years of service, so it would seem that it had been a veritable struggle to see who would come out on top. This was pitting the two arch deceivers against each other, and it was like the world cup final to see who would win.

Laban didn't stand a chance, though, as he was not pitted against Jacob but God. Chapter 31 v 12 clarifies that God's work resulted in the best of the cattle being turned over to Jacob. It didn't matter how many times Laban changed Jacob's wages. God simply altered the outcome.

Jacob wanted to return to the promised land initially but was constrained by Laban to stay. It was apparent to Laban that Jacob's presence had blessed him, and he did want Jacob to go.

There were probably some elements of coercion and threats involved to make Jacob stay as well. In the narrative that follows, Jacob is seen as afraid of Laban, especially in leaving the area, so much that he had to sneak away.

The methods that Jacob used were linked in some way to the health, wellbeing and reproduction of the cattle, but overall it was God's hand that directed the outcome. Studies in recent times have shown some medicinal benefits in using the particular trees which Jacob used.

Many Christians act this way and justify it by saying that their Christian lives and secular lives are apart. However, if we are Christian, every part of our lives involve and reflect on our character. It is simply never good enough to behave in this way.

If we find ourselves in a situation where we are faced with this type of behaviour, it is better to walk away rather than respond in kind. If we cannot walk away, then we should pray to God for a solution. Never respond in the same manner as this destroys our testimony.

If God is for us, then anything the world throws at us will come out in our favour, regardless of how hard the world tries to change that. So to take steps to change things in our own way, we are simply showing our unbelief in the ability of God to fulfil what he has promised.

CHAPTER 11

Jacob Flees Again

Genesis 31:1-21

Jacob heard that Laban's sons were saying, "Jacob has taken everything our father owned and has gained all this wealth from what belonged to our father." And Jacob noticed that Laban's attitude toward him was not what it had been.

Then the Lord said to Jacob, "Go back to the land of your fathers and to your relatives, and I will be with you."

So Jacob sent word to Rachel and Leah to come out to the fields where his flocks were. He said to them, "I see that your father's attitude toward me is not what it was before, but the God of my father has been with me. You know that I've worked for your father with all my strength, yet your father has cheated me by changing my wages ten times. However, God has not allowed him to harm me. If he said, 'The speckled ones will be your wages,' then all the flocks gave birth to speckled young; and if he said, 'The streaked ones will be your wages,' then all the flocks bore streaked young. So God has taken away your father's livestock and has given them to me.

"In breeding season I once had a dream in which I looked up and saw that the male goats mating with the flock were streaked, speckled or spot-

ted. The angel of God said to me in the dream, 'Jacob.' I answered, 'Here I am.' And he said, 'Look up and see that all the male goats mating with the flock are streaked, speckled or spotted, for I have seen all that Laban has been doing to you. I am the God of Bethel, where you anointed a pillar and where you made a vow to me. Now leave this land at once and go back to your native land.'"

Then Rachel and Leah replied, "Do we still have any share in the inheritance of our father's estate? Does he not regard us as foreigners? Not only has he sold us, but he has used up what was paid for us. Surely all the wealth that God took away from our father belongs to us and our children. So do whatever God has told you."

Then Jacob put his children and his wives on camels, and he drove all his livestock ahead of him, along with all the goods he had accumulated in Paddan Aram, to go to his father Isaac in the land of Canaan.

When Laban had gone to shear his sheep, Rachel stole her father's household gods. Moreover, Jacob deceived Laban the Aramean by not telling him he was running away. So he fled with all he had, crossed the Euphrates River, and headed for the hill country of Gilead.

Everything comes to a head. Laban had tried every trick in the book, had changed Jacob's wages ten times, but every time he tried to get the upper hand, God thwarted him. Laban and his sons are now getting angry about what they perceived to be an injustice against them by Jacob, and the situation was becoming dangerous.

Jacob decides it is time to go and readies all his family, his flocks and his possessions. An opportune time arrives when Laban is away shearing sheep, and Jacob flees with everything he has. But, unfortunately, he also leaves, unwittingly, with something which is not his.

The godless idolatry has not left these two sisters, and Rachel steals Laban's household gods. Given that God hates idolatry, we would wonder how he could allow this and, indeed, would he allow this to happen without consequences. Also, does Rachel's inability to have children have anything to do with her idolatry?

Twenty years of service comes to an end and not very amicably. Yet, despite twenty years of working together, or maybe we should say, because of twenty years working together, they do not trust each other.

What would our Christian testimony be if those around us cannot trust us? Yet, it happens all the time in Christian circles. Sadly, many Christians are no different from unbelievers in their business dealings and have no testimony to present before men.

It is always challenging as a Christian if someone else is not being honest with you, but we must try as best as we can to remain fair, even if it costs us. Over the past seven years, Laban has not been honest with Jacob, but it perhaps worked both ways.

Certainly, Laban's sons seem to believe they had got the wrong end of the bargain. Indeed, they had, but that was God's design, rather than as a result of Jacob's manipulation, although that may have played a part too.

Everything is working together here, which is not surprising since God was directing the outcome. Just as Laban's family are getting angry, God tells Jacob it is time to go home. Interestingly enough, this is only the second time we hear God talking to Jacob and the first time in twenty years.

It is revealing that even though we live outside God's influence for years and years, he is still looking out for us and help us. Interestingly, Jacob does not tell his wives that God spoke to him, merely citing their father's attitude towards him for the reason. He does seem to have to convince them, though. Then, finally, perhaps when they are not confident, he tells them God has spoken to him.

As soon as his wives agreed, Jacob jumped into action and left the very same day, eager to be away before his father-in-law returned. But, once again, Jacob's behaviour had caught up with him, and he has to flee.

As Christians, we should realise that although God may protect us and look out for us, there will still be consequences for us if we misbehave.

Often those consequences may be as simple as we are not fit to take an official place within our local Church, but at other times, they may well be much more severe as God will not protect us from the consequences of breaking the country's law.

CHAPTER 12

Treaty with Laban

Genesis 31:22-55

On the third day Laban was told that Jacob had fled. Taking his relatives with him, he pursued Jacob for seven days and caught up with him in the hill country of Gilead. Then God came to Laban the Aramean in a dream at night and said to him, "Be careful not to say anything to Jacob, either good or bad."

Jacob had pitched his tent in the hill country of Gilead when Laban overtook him, and Laban and his relatives camped there too. Then Laban said to Jacob, "What have you done? You've deceived me, and you've carried off my daughters like captives in war. Why did you run off secretly and deceive me? Why didn't you tell me, so I could send you away with joy and singing to the music of timbrels and harps? You didn't even let me kiss my grandchildren and my daughters goodbye. You have done a foolish thing. I have the power to harm you; but last night the God of your father said to me, 'Be careful not to say anything to Jacob, either good or bad.' Now you have gone off because you longed to return to your father's household. But why did you steal my gods?"

Jacob answered Laban, "I was afraid, because I thought you would take your daughters away from me by force. But if you find anyone who has your gods, that person shall not live. In the presence of our relatives, see for yourself whether there is anything of yours here with me; and if so, take it." Now Jacob did not know that Rachel had stolen the gods.

So Laban went into Jacob's tent and into Leah's tent and into the tent of the two female servants, but he found nothing. After he came out of Leah's tent, he entered Rachel's tent. Now Rachel had taken the household gods and put them inside her camel's saddle and was sitting on them. Laban searched through everything in the tent but found nothing.

Rachel said to her father, "Don't be angry, my lord, that I cannot stand up in your presence; I'm having my period." So he searched but could not find the household gods.

Jacob was angry and took Laban to task. "What is my crime?" he asked Laban. "How have I wronged you that you hunt me down? Now that you have searched through all my goods, what have you found that belongs to your household? Put it here in front of your relatives and mine, and let them judge between the two of us.

"I have been with you for twenty years now. Your sheep and goats have not miscarried, nor have I eaten rams from your flocks. I did not bring you animals torn by wild beasts; I bore the loss myself. And you demanded payment from me for whatever was stolen by day or night. This was my situation: The heat consumed me in the daytime and the cold at night, and sleep fled from my eyes. It was like this for the twenty years I was in your household. I worked for you fourteen years for your two daughters and six years for your flocks, and you changed my wages ten times. If the God of my father, the God of Abraham and the Fear of Isaac, had not been with me, you would surely have sent me away empty-handed. But God has seen my hardship and the toil of my hands, and last night he rebuked you."

Laban answered Jacob, "The women are my daughters, the children are my children, and the flocks are my flocks. All you see is mine. Yet what can

I do today about these daughters of mine, or about the children they have borne? Come now, let's make a covenant, you and I, and let it serve as a witness between us."

So Jacob took a stone and set it up as a pillar. He said to his relatives, "Gather some stones." So they took stones and piled them in a heap, and they ate there by the heap. Laban called it Jegar Sahadutha, and Jacob called it Galeed.

Laban said, "This heap is a witness between you and me today." That is why it was called Galeed. It was also called Mizpah, because he said, "May the Lord keep watch between you and me when we are away from each other. If you mistreat my daughters or if you take any wives besides my daughters, even though no one is with us, remember that God is a witness between you and me."

Laban also said to Jacob, "Here is this heap, and here is this pillar I have set up between you and me. This heap is a witness, and this pillar is a witness, that I will not go past this heap to your side to harm you and that you will not go past this heap and pillar to my side to harm me. May the God of Abraham and the God of Nahor, the God of their father, judge between us."

So Jacob took an oath in the name of the Fear of his father Isaac. He offered a sacrifice there in the hill country and invited his relatives to a meal. After they had eaten, they spent the night there.

Early the next morning Laban kissed his grandchildren and his daughters and blessed them. Then he left and returned home.

Jacob must have been moving fast. To cover around three hundred miles in ten days with large flocks is no mean feat. It was three days before Laban found out they were gone, and then he pursued them for a further seven days before he caught up with them three hundred miles to the south.

It would seem, by the narrative, that Laban did intend to take action against Jacob, had not God intervened and warned him against this course. Of course, Laban was not a believer in God, but over the past twenty years, he had seen how God protected and blessed Jacob and would have been afraid to act when God had explicitly warned him.

Laban was not happy, though, particularly since his household gods had been stolen. So he searched the entire camp without finding them as Rachel had cunningly hidden them.

In the end, they make a covenant, but it is more of a warning rather than friendship, as it contained penalties if the other party were to cross over the boundary.

Many have taken Mizpah to mean that God will watch carefully over the other party while they are parted from one another temporarily. Nothing could be further from the truth. The true meaning is that God will call down wrath on the other party if they violate this treaty by straying onto the other's territory.

The two parties agreed not to cross over this boundary and then spent the night having one last meal together before parting directions.

There is a growing sense of unease here as we learn more about Rachel. Jacob loved her and was sent to Haran to get a wife rather than have a wife from the Godless tribes around them, but we see increasingly that Rachel was not much better than the Canaanite women.

Rachel had stolen from her father, and to make matters worse, it was his household gods she had stolen. Rachel valued these as something worth stealing, which set her at odds against God's plan. Something not very good will come of this.

Another interesting point in this narrative that points to Jacob's change is that we now see Jacob offering a sacrifice to God for the first time in his life. Thus, little by little, God has changed Jacob from the deceiver....to what?

CHAPTER 13

Jacob Bargains with God

Jacob Bargains with God
Genesis 32:1-21

Jacob also went on his way, and the angels of God met him. When Jacob saw them, he said, "This is the camp of God!" So he named that place Mahanaim.

Jacob sent messengers ahead of him to his brother Esau in the land of Seir, the country of Edom. He instructed them: "This is what you are to say to my lord Esau: 'Your servant Jacob says, I have been staying with Laban and have remained there till now. I have cattle and donkeys, sheep and goats, male and female servants. Now I am sending this message to my lord, that I may find favor in your eyes.'"

When the messengers returned to Jacob, they said, "We went to your brother Esau, and now he is coming to meet you, and four hundred men are with him."

In great fear and distress Jacob divided the people who were with him into two groups, and the flocks and herds and camels as well. He thought, "If Esau comes and attacks one group, the group that is left may escape."

Then Jacob prayed, "O God of my father Abraham, God of my father Isaac, Lord, you who said to me, 'Go back to your country and your relatives, and I will make you prosper,' I am unworthy of all the kindness and faithfulness you have shown your servant. I had only my staff when I crossed this Jordan, but now I have become two camps. Save me, I pray, from the hand of my brother Esau, for I am afraid he will come and attack me, and also the mothers with their children. But you have said, 'I will surely make you prosper and will make your descendants like the sand of the sea, which cannot be counted.'"

He spent the night there, and from what he had with him he selected a gift for his brother Esau: two hundred female goats and twenty male goats, two hundred ewes and twenty rams, thirty female camels with their young, forty cows and ten bulls, and twenty female donkeys and ten male donkeys. He put them in the care of his servants, each herd by itself, and said to his servants, "Go ahead of me, and keep some space between the herds."

He instructed the one in the lead: "When my brother Esau meets you and asks, 'Who do you belong to, and where are you going, and who owns all these animals in front of you?' then you are to say, 'They belong to your servant Jacob. They are a gift sent to my lord Esau, and he is coming behind us.'"

He also instructed the second, the third and all the others who followed the herds: "You are to say the same thing to Esau when you meet him. And be sure to say, 'Your servant Jacob is coming behind us.'" For he thought, "I will pacify him with these gifts I am sending on ahead; later, when I see him, perhaps he will receive me." So Jacob's gifts went on ahead of him, but he himself spent the night in the camp.

It would seem that Jacob is leaving one crisis to face another. He has escaped one dangerous enemy to face another. After his covenant with

Laban, he does not have the option of turning back, so he must go forward to meet Esau, who had wanted to kill him twenty years previously when he left this area.

Jacob remembers this only too well. He was alone when he fled twenty years previously, so no one else in his camp appreciates the danger they are now facing. Jacob prepares gifts for his brother to try and appease him. The size of the gifts gives us some idea of how wealthy he was by this time.

The messengers he had sent to Esau return with the message that Esau is coming with four hundred men to meet him, and Jacob is sent into terror. He prepares for the worst and splits his band so that if Esau attacks one camp, the other can escape.

He then turns to the one he should have turned to long before and prays to God for protection. He reminds God of all his promises and that God himself had sent on this journey. Thus, the picture we have here is of a terrified Jacob, pleading with God to save him from what he sees as certain death and obliteration.

Are we like this? Do we carry out our own plans and only turn to God when we get in trouble? I know I am guilty of that. The truth is that God wants a relationship with us all the time, not just when we are in trouble. Also, it is a lack of faith if we feel we must do things in our own way. It implies that God cannot or will not do what he says.

Another sign of the change in Jacob is that he is met by angels here. Unfortunately, there is no narrative to tell us what went on between Jacob and the angels, but it surely must have been a momentous occasion as Jacob names the area for the meeting as God's camp.

Jacob now finally comes to the place where he accepts that God is sovereign and can give and take away, can build up or pull down. Jacob is not quite sure which one is his lot, but he does remember well the promises God made.

When we are in trouble, we will do well to remember God's promises. We may well be the same as Jacob, we do not deserve God's kindness in our lives, but God is faithful, even though we are not. He will always hold to his word, even if we do not.

CHAPTER 14

The Deceiver Turns Winner

<u>The Deceiver Turns Winner</u>
Genesis 32:22-32

That night Jacob got up and took his two wives, his two female servants and his eleven sons and crossed the ford of the Jabbok. After he had sent them across the stream, he sent over all his possessions. So Jacob was left alone, and a man wrestled with him till daybreak. When the man saw that he could not overpower him, he touched the socket of Jacob's hip so that his hip was wrenched as he wrestled with the man. Then the man said, "Let me go, for it is daybreak."

But Jacob replied, "I will not let you go unless you bless me."

The man asked him, "What is your name?"

"Jacob," he answered.

Then the man said, "Your name will no longer be Jacob, but Israel, because you have struggled with God and with humans and have overcome."

Jacob said, "Please tell me your name."

But he replied, "Why do you ask my name?" Then he blessed him there.

So Jacob called the place Peniel, saying, "It is because I saw God face to face, and yet my life was spared."

The sun rose above him as he passed Peniel, and he was limping because of his hip. Therefore to this day the Israelites do not eat the tendon attached to the socket of the hip, because the socket of Jacob's hip was touched near the tendon.

The stories get stranger and stranger if we look from a worldly viewpoint, but we cannot look from an earthly perspective here as this was a spiritual encounter.

It is usually when you are on your own, at the end of your own resources, when God steps in, and this is the point Jacob had reached.

Jacob had done well for himself and had acquired great earthly treasures, but at this point, it wasn't very important. He had sent it all from him, and it was all in danger of being taken from him, and he was left alone.

He has turned to God for help, acknowledging that everything is dependent on God, and this is the place where God can help. Jacob feels like he is at the end of himself and needs help, so when he encounters the man in the story, he will not let the man go until the man blesses him.

Jacob is well aware that this is no ordinary man and that this represents God himself. He wrestles all night with the man but will not let him go. Jacob is only too aware that he needs God's blessing, and he is not giving up until he gets what he wants.

Finally, when Dawn arrives, and Jacob will still not let the man go, the man blesses Jacob and tells him that his name has changed from Jacob to Israel. Jacob was the deceiver, but Israel means something like a winner. The name indicates that Jacob has struggled all night and has prevailed, so the winner seems applicable.

Have you reached this point in your life yet where only God can help you? Have you attained the point where you pray and present your petitions to him and will not let go until he answers you and blesses you?

What characterises a person who has reached this point? They care not for anything else compared to the blessing they must have from God. Everything else in their life is worthless compared to what God has promised them. They firmly believe that God will deliver, but they know, in their heart, that he will only answer when they come to him one hundred percent.

So many times in my life, I have wanted what God has for me, but I was not quite willing to give up what I already held. It just doesn't work. If you're going to be in the centre of God's will, then everything else must go on the altar. Just as Jacob sent everything away from him and stayed alone with God, so must we do the same.

CHAPTER 15

Jacob and Esau Reconcile

<u>Jacob and Esau Reconcile</u>
Genesis 33:1-20

Jacob looked up and there was Esau, coming with his four hundred men; so he divided the children among Leah, Rachel and the two female servants. He put the female servants and their children in front, Leah and her children next, and Rachel and Joseph in the rear. He himself went on ahead and bowed down to the ground seven times as he approached his brother.

But Esau ran to meet Jacob and embraced him; he threw his arms around his neck and kissed him. And they wept. Then Esau looked up and saw the women and children. "Who are these with you?" he asked.

Jacob answered, "They are the children God has graciously given your servant."

Then the female servants and their children approached and bowed down. Next, Leah and her children came and bowed down. Last of all came Joseph and Rachel, and they too bowed down.

Esau asked, "What's the meaning of all these flocks and herds I met?"

"To find favor in your eyes, my lord," he said.

But Esau said, "I already have plenty, my brother. Keep what you have for yourself."

"No, please!" said Jacob. "If I have found favor in your eyes, accept this gift from me. For to see your face is like seeing the face of God, now that you have received me favorably. Please accept the present that was brought to you, for God has been gracious to me and I have all I need." And because Jacob insisted, Esau accepted it.

Then Esau said, "Let us be on our way; I'll accompany you."

But Jacob said to him, "My lord knows that the children are tender and that I must care for the ewes and cows that are nursing their young. If they are driven hard just one day, all the animals will die. So let my lord go on ahead of his servant, while I move along slowly at the pace of the flocks and herds before me and the pace of the children, until I come to my lord in Seir."

Esau said, "Then let me leave some of my men with you."

"But why do that?" Jacob asked. "Just let me find favor in the eyes of my lord."

So that day Esau started on his way back to Seir. Jacob, however, went to Sukkoth, where he built a place for himself and made shelters for his livestock. That is why the place is called Sukkoth.

After Jacob came from Paddan Aram, he arrived safely at the city of Shechem in Canaan and camped within sight of the city. For a hundred pieces of silver, he bought from the sons of Hamor, the father of Shechem, the plot of ground where he pitched his tent. There he set up an altar and called it El Elohe Israel.

Jacob finally arrives and meets Esau. He is apprehensive about how the meeting will go and sets out his family to escape in the event of trouble. Still, his preparations were unnecessary as Esau has no bad feelings towards his brother.

Esau seems to have forgotten all about their fight from twenty years before. It appears to be a trait that Esau has, to forgive quickly and put troubles behind him. He rushes to Jacob, and they embrace with Esau, delighted to see his brother.

It also seems that Esau has faired just as well as Jacob has and has no need for Jacob's gifts. He is glad to see his brother, and there is no thought now in Esau's mind of revenge. It is all forgotten about and in the past.

Jacob is relieved to find his brother so favourably disposed towards him and presses his brother to accept the gifts. They part on good terms and go to their own places. Jacob buys a parcel of land to pitch his tent. He then builds an altar to God. Jacob has become a changed man.

It would seem that Jacob's transformation is complete, and he has now adopted his grandfather's practice of building altars. He is also finally putting down roots and buys the ground around him for a permanent settlement.

However, I am not convinced that everything is OK between the two brothers. Jacob is wary, and having told Esau he would travel to Seir, he now makes no effort to do this at all and is very insistent that Esau does not leave any of his men around.

Esau seemed to be genuinely glad to see Jacob, and this does fit in with his character that he forgives easily. But, on the other hand, perhaps Jacob is feeling guilty and still not comfortable with his past mistakes.

Some errors we make in life can be forgiven, but often it is more difficult to forget, and some mistakes from our past will continue to dog us throughout our lives.

CHAPTER 16

Dinah's Shame Revenged

Genesis 34:1-31
Now Dinah, the daughter Leah had borne to Jacob, went out to visit the women of the land. When Shechem son of Hamor the Hivite, the ruler of that area, saw her, he took her and raped her. His heart was drawn to Dinah daughter of Jacob; he loved the young woman and spoke tenderly to her. And Shechem said to his father Hamor, "Get me this girl as my wife."

When Jacob heard that his daughter Dinah had been defiled, his sons were in the fields with his livestock; so he did nothing about it until they came home.

Then Shechem's father Hamor went out to talk with Jacob. Meanwhile, Jacob's sons had come in from the fields as soon as they heard what had happened. They were shocked and furious, because Shechem had done an outrageous thing in Israel by sleeping with Jacob's daughter—a thing that should not be done.

But Hamor said to them, "My son Shechem has his heart set on your daughter. Please give her to him as his wife. Intermarry with us; give us your daughters and take our daughters for yourselves. You can settle among us; the land is open to you. Live in it, trade in it, and acquire property in it."

Then Shechem said to Dinah's father and brothers, "Let me find favor in your eyes, and I will give you whatever you ask. Make the price for the bride and the gift I am to bring as great as you like, and I'll pay whatever you ask me. Only give me the young woman as my wife."

Because their sister Dinah had been defiled, Jacob's sons replied deceitfully as they spoke to Shechem and his father Hamor. They said to them, "We can't do such a thing; we can't give our sister to a man who is not circumcised. That would be a disgrace to us. We will enter into an agreement with you on one condition only: that you become like us by circumcising all your males. Then we will give you our daughters and take your daughters for ourselves. We'll settle among you and become one people with you. But if you will not agree to be circumcised, we'll take our sister and go."

Their proposal seemed good to Hamor and his son Shechem. The young man, who was the most honored of all his father's family, lost no time in doing what they said, because he was delighted with Jacob's daughter. So Hamor and his son Shechem went to the gate of their city to speak to the men of their city. "These men are friendly toward us," they said. "Let them live in our land and trade in it; the land has plenty of room for them. We can marry their daughters and they can marry ours. But the men will agree to live with us as one people only on the condition that our males be circumcised, as they themselves are. Won't their livestock, their property and all their other animals become ours? So let us agree to their terms, and they will settle among us."

All the men who went out of the city gate agreed with Hamor and his son Shechem, and every male in the city was circumcised.

Three days later, while all of them were still in pain, two of Jacob's sons, Simeon and Levi, Dinah's brothers, took their swords and attacked the unsuspecting city, killing every male. They put Hamor and his son Shechem to the sword and took Dinah from Shechem's house and left. The sons of Jacob *came upon the dead bodies and looted the city where their sister had been defiled. They seized their flocks and herds and donkeys and everything else of theirs in the city and out in the fields. They carried off all their wealth and all their women and children, taking as plunder everything in the houses.*

Then Jacob said to Simeon and Levi, "You have brought trouble on me by making me obnoxious to the Canaanites and Perizzites, the people living in this land. We are few in number, and if they join forces against me and attack me, I and my household will be destroyed."

But they replied, "Should he have treated our sister like a prostitute?"

Here we have a typical spoiled kid, son of the king, who has always been able to get his own way. Now he pushes it a bit too far and to the wrong people. He picks on the wrong people and pays the ultimate price for his grievous harm against Dinah.

Jacob's sons have the same traits as Jacob had, and they trick the locals into disabling themselves so that they can be more easily killed. Two of Jacob's sons kill all the men in the city and ransack the city and take away all the women, children, and goods found there.

Jacob is worried about how this will work out, but the sons are adamant that they cannot allow anyone to treat their sister this way and get off with it. It would seem Jacob is getting more like his father, Isaac, and the sons are becoming like Jacob in his youth.

It was, without a doubt, a terrible thing which they did to Dinah, but was the revenge justified. We will come upon issues like this all through our Christian life, and the question is always, do we fight back, or do we turn the other cheek?

It is a tough question, and I would suggest the answer is to do what they didn't do here. Talk to God about it. Remember back when God was going to destroy Sodom and Abraham was very disturbed about it? He made his feelings known to God, and God worked out a solution.

When we are in challenging situations and don't know what to do, it is always time to head for the throne of grace. To not consult God but rush out and act very often ends in trouble. We may see everything as black and white, but God always sees the big picture and sees things hidden from us. He always has more solutions than we do.

CHAPTER 17

Return to Bethel

<u>Return to Bethel</u>
Genesis 35:1-15

Then God said to Jacob, "Go up to Bethel and settle there, and build an altar there to God, who appeared to you when you were fleeing from your brother Esau."

So Jacob said to his household and to all who were with him, "Get rid of the foreign gods you have with you, and purify yourselves and change your clothes. Then come, let us go up to Bethel, where I will build an altar to God, who answered me in the day of my distress and who has been with me wherever I have gone." So they gave Jacob all the foreign gods they had and the rings in their ears, and Jacob buried them under the oak at Shechem. Then they set out, and the terror of God fell on the towns all around them so that no one pursued them.

Jacob and all the people with him came to Luz (that is, Bethel) in the land of Canaan. There he built an altar, and he called the place El Bethel, because it was there that God revealed himself to him when he was fleeing from his brother.

Now Deborah, Rebekah's nurse, died and was buried under the oak outside Bethel. So it was named Allon Bakuth.

After Jacob returned from Paddan Aram, God appeared to him again and blessed him. God said to him, "Your name is Jacob, but you will no longer be called Jacob; your name will be Israel." So he named him Israel.

And God said to him, "I am God Almighty; be fruitful and increase in number. A nation and a community of nations will come from you, and kings will be among your descendants. The land I gave to Abraham and Isaac I also give to you, and I will give this land to your descendants after you." Then God went up from him at the place where he had talked with him.

Jacob set up a stone pillar at the place where God had talked with him, and he poured out a drink offering on it; he also poured oil on it. Jacob called the place where God had talked with him Bethel.

Bethel, The House of God. Jacob had come a long way since he last visited this place over twenty years previously. At that time, it was the first time he had encountered God for himself. It had not been an immediate change, but God had worked on him gradually over the twenty years and had completed a transformation of the rogue into a winner.

When God calls Jacob to return to Bethel, Jacob is very aware that he is being called to a holy place. Until this point, he had tolerated the false gods and extravagances of his household, but he knows that can no longer be allowed. He knows that the family cannot go to the house of God until they purify themselves.

Jacob and his family purify themselves and bury their old attachments and habits. They then proceed to Bethel, and the change in their status is noticeable to all around them. All the people around them were in complete terror and kept out of their way. Yes, they had slaughtered the men in Shechem, but it was more than that. The neighbours could see that God was with them.

When they arrive in Bethel, Jacob builds an altar to God and worships him. God appears again to Jacob and confirms his promise, and even commands Jacob to be fruitful and multiply.

This is a lesson for all because, at some point, we all get the call to the house of God. When we get the call to the house of God, we must rid ourselves of all our attachments and habits and purify ourselves to meet God.

When we are called to the house of God, it is not just a routine visit to Church, but a solemn occasion when we are recognised as ministers of God in some capacity. This may be as a Pastor, or it may simply be as a cleaning lady for the Church, but if God calls us to a position, it doesn't matter what that position is, as every member is the same in God's eyes, and it is where God wants you to be.

Whatever God calls us to, he will fit us for and give us the resources we need. All we need to do is stay close to him, and to do this, we need to purify ourselves.

CHAPTER 18

Death of Rachel

<u>Death of Rachel</u>
Genesis 35:16-21
Then they moved on from Bethel. While they were still some distance from Ephrath, Rachel began to give birth and had great difficulty. And as she was having great difficulty in childbirth, the midwife said to her, "Don't despair, for you have another son." As she breathed her last—for she was dying—she named her son Ben-Oni. But his father named him Benjamin.
So Rachel died and was buried on the way to Ephrath (that is, Bethlehem). Over her tomb Jacob set up a pillar, and to this day that pillar marks Rachel's tomb.
Israel moved on again and pitched his tent beyond Migdal

Going to the house of God, worshipping God and being blessed by God does not exempt Jacob from troubles and trials. They have barely moved on, and his beloved Rachel, whom he loved, died giving birth to her second son.

This would have been a big blow to Jacob and Rachel's other son, Joseph, who would be only a few years old. Rachel, as she was dying, named her son Ben-oni, which means son of my distress. Jacob, however, changes the name and names him Benjamin, the son of my right hand. Jacob always retained his optimism, regardless of what surrounded him.

We cannot help but wonder why Rachel had this trouble. Was it related to the false Gods she held onto? Was this the price for her unbelief?

It is always difficult in a relationship where one partner is an unbeliever. It causes unimaginable distress, and any young unmarried people need to read this and take this onboard to choose a life partner wisely.

For those already married to an unbeliever, Paul gives great counsel in this situation in 1st Corinthians chapter 7. The general line is if the other party is happy to stay together, then you should not be the one to break it up, but pray for your partner.

An unbelieving mother can have a considerable influence on the children, which we need to bring to God. This certainly didn't seem to be a problem with Rebekah's children, as Joseph became better than all the other brothers. Perhaps this was because Rachel died while he was still very young and did not have the same influence on him.

CHAPTER 19

Joseph Lost

<u>Joseph Lost</u>
Genesis 37:12-36
Now his brothers had gone to graze their father's flocks near Shechem, and Israel said to Joseph, "As you know, your brothers are grazing the flocks near Shechem. Come, I am going to send you to them."

"Very well," he replied.

So he said to him, "Go and see if all is well with your brothers and with the flocks, and bring word back to me." Then he sent him off from the Valley of Hebron.

When Joseph arrived at Shechem, a man found him wandering around in the fields and asked him, "What are you looking for?"

He replied, "I'm looking for my brothers. Can you tell me where they are grazing their flocks?"

"They have moved on from here," the man answered. "I heard them say, 'Let's go to Dothan.'"

So Joseph went after his brothers and found them near Dothan. But they saw him in the distance, and before he reached them, they plotted to kill him.

"Here comes that dreamer!" they said to each other. "Come now, let's kill him and throw him into one of these cisterns and say that a ferocious animal devoured him. Then we'll see what comes of his dreams."

When Reuben heard this, he tried to rescue him from their hands. "Let's not take his life," he said. "Don't shed any blood. Throw him into this cistern here in the wilderness, but don't lay a hand on him." Reuben said this to rescue him from them and take him back to his father.

So when Joseph came to his brothers, they stripped him of his robe—the ornate robe he was wearing— and they took him and threw him into the cistern. The cistern was empty; there was no water in it.

As they sat down to eat their meal, they looked up and saw a caravan of Ishmaelites coming from Gilead. Their camels were loaded with spices, balm and myrrh, and they were on their way to take them down to Egypt.

Judah said to his brothers, "What will we gain if we kill our brother and cover up his blood? Come, let's sell him to the Ishmaelites and not lay our hands on him; after all, he is our brother, our own flesh and blood." His brothers agreed.

So when the Midianite merchants came by, his brothers pulled Joseph up out of the cistern and sold him for twenty shekels of silver to the Ishmaelites, who took him to Egypt.

When Reuben returned to the cistern and saw that Joseph was not there, he tore his clothes. He went back to his brothers and said, "The boy isn't there! Where can I turn now?"

Then they got Joseph's robe, slaughtered a goat and dipped the robe in the blood. They took the ornate robe back to their father and said, "We found this. Examine it to see whether it is your son's robe."

He recognized it and said, "It is my son's robe! Some ferocious animal has devoured him. Joseph has surely been torn to pieces."

Then Jacob tore his clothes, put on sackcloth and mourned for his son many days. All his sons and daughters came to comfort him, but he refused to be comforted. "No," he said, "I will continue to mourn until I join my son in the grave." So his father wept for him.

Meanwhile, the Midianites sold Joseph in Egypt to Potiphar, one of Pharaoh's officials, the captain of the guard.

We skipped a few chapters which gave us the story of how Joseph annoyed his brothers. Although perhaps annoyed is not strong enough, they hated him enough to kill him. Jacob also thought that Joseph was out of place but couldn't quite shake what Joseph was saying.

Joseph was Jacob's favourite, carrying on his father and mother's trait, favouring one of their children. Unfortunately, Jacob made it worse by treating Joseph differently, giving him preferential treatment over the other ten boys.

There comes a time when the boys are growing older, most of them into their twenties, and they are away in the fields grazing their sheep. Jacob sends Joseph to see how they are, bring them some provisions, and report back. The brothers immediately see their opportunity to be rid of this loathsome creature who continually annoyed them.

Reuben is the only one with a conscience, and he saved Joseph from being killed. But, unfortunately, Reuben had to go away somewhere, and when he returned, the brothers had sold Joseph into slavery. Reuben was distraught by this turn of events but does go along with the deception they now plan.

The brothers return home to their father and present Joseph's coat, which Jacob recognises at once. The brothers have smeared it with blood and convinced their father that Joseph is dead.

Jacob is distraught and refuses to be comforted. He declares that he will mourn all the remainder of his days until he joins his son in death.

Here we thought Jacob had got his act together, and it was all happy families when the situation was even worse than it was between Jacob and Esau years ago. But, once again, we see God's sovereign choice come into play and being rejected by others.

Although God had not personally appeared to Joseph, God had chosen him, and his dreams confirmed this. The boys did not see this, but Jacob did have an inkling that God was at work. Jacob had learned a lot, but the sons still had much to learn.

Can we relate to that? I certainly can. When I was young, I thought I knew it all, but now at the ripe old age of 62, I know differently. When I look back over my life, my biggest mistake was thinking I was running the show, when all the time, God was in control.

How do we, as Christians, react when tragedy strikes us? Are we like Jacob, who determines to mourn all his days or do we turn everything over to our father in heaven who knows everything and trust Him for the outcome?

It's a hard thing, of that there is no doubt, but if we look back, we can see God's hand in our lives, guiding and protecting us. Why would he stop now? Our call must always be Ebenezer (This far, the Lord has helped me).

CHAPTER 20

Joseph Found

<u>Joseph Found</u>
Genesis 45:1-13 & 25-28

Then Joseph could no longer control himself before all his attendants, and he cried out, "Have everyone leave my presence!" So there was no one with Joseph when he made himself known to his brothers. And he wept so loudly that the Egyptians heard him, and Pharaoh's household heard about it.

Joseph said to his brothers, "I am Joseph! Is my father still living?" But his brothers were not able to answer him, because they were terrified at his presence.

Then Joseph said to his brothers, "Come close to me." When they had done so, he said, "I am your brother Joseph, the one you sold into Egypt! And now, do not be distressed and do not be angry with yourselves for selling me here, because it was to save lives that God sent me ahead of you. For two years now there has been famine in the land, and for the next five years there will be no plowing and reaping. But God sent me ahead of you to preserve for you a remnant on earth and to save your lives by a great deliverance.

"So then, it was not you who sent me here, but God. He made me father to Pharaoh, lord of his entire household and ruler of all Egypt. Now hurry back to my father and say to him, 'This is what your son Joseph says: God has made me lord of all Egypt. Come down to me; don't delay. You shall live in the region of Goshen and be near me—you, your children and grandchildren, your flocks and herds, and all you have. I will provide for you there, because five years of famine are still to come. Otherwise you and your household and all who belong to you will become destitute.'

"You can see for yourselves, and so can my brother Benjamin, that it is really I who am speaking to you. Tell my father about all the honor accorded me in Egypt and about everything you have seen. And bring my father down here quickly."

So they went up out of Egypt and came to their father Jacob in the land of Canaan. They told him, "Joseph is still alive! In fact, he is ruler of all Egypt." Jacob was stunned; he did not believe them. But when they told him everything Joseph had said to them, and when he saw the carts Joseph had sent to carry him back, the spirit of their father Jacob revived. And Israel said, "I'm convinced! My son Joseph is still alive. I will go and see him before I die."

We have skipped fifteen years here since there was no narrative on Jacob. Much has taken place for Joseph in this period, and you would do well to read the chapter between these two parts. Joseph has progressed from the lowest slave in Egypt, via the prison, to the second-highest ruler in the land.

The brothers are stunned and terrified of the revenge which would be sure to come upon them now. They were very much aware that they had wronged Joseph, and there was now a dawning on them that Joseph held the power of life and death over them.

However, Joseph can see the bigger picture and can rightly observe that being sold as a slave into Egypt was all part of God's plan to preserve his family and grow them from a family into a nation. Moreover, Joseph sees his position now as being able to assist in this plan. Thus, he does not see that it was the brother's fault, selling him into slavery, but rather that it was God's plan.

Joseph manages to calm and convince the brothers that he means them no harm, indeed that he seeks to help them. He gives them everything they need to go back to Canaan and bring his father down to Egypt, along with everything he possesses, where they will all be protected from the famine that would rage for a further five years.

Jacob can barely believe the story the brothers relate to him, but the goods and carts Joseph sent convince him it must be true. Jacob had been mourning for fifteen years but now is immediately revived and determines to go to Egypt and see Joseph for himself.

There are two fundamental lessons for us here. Firstly, we need to strive to be more like Joseph, forgiving and helpful. Also, like Joseph, we should see the bigger picture and endeavour to help those in the world around us. This will display Jesus much more than our words could ever do.

Secondly, we need to realise that nothing is impossible for God. That which we think is lost forever need not be so with God. We often look at the lost and believe some can never, ever be found or saved. This is not true, and there is no one God cannot reach. We must never despair of any situation while our God is on the throne.

CHAPTER 21

Down to Egypt

Genesis 46:1-7 & 28-34
So Israel set out with all that was his, and when he reached Beersheba, he offered sacrifices to the God of his father Isaac.
And God spoke to Israel in a vision at night and said, "Jacob! Jacob!"
"Here I am," he replied.
"I am God, the God of your father," he said. "Do not be afraid to go down to Egypt, for I will make you into a great nation there. I will go down to Egypt with you, and I will surely bring you back again. And Joseph's own hand will close your eyes."
Then Jacob left Beersheba, and Israel's sons took their father Jacob and their children and their wives in the carts that Pharaoh had sent to transport him. So Jacob and all his offspring went to Egypt, taking with them their livestock and the possessions they had acquired in Canaan. Jacob brought with him to Egypt his sons and grandsons and his daughters and granddaughters—all his offspring.
Now Jacob sent Judah ahead of him to Joseph to get directions to Goshen. When they arrived in the region of Goshen, Joseph had his chariot made ready and went to Goshen to meet his father Israel. As soon as Joseph ap-

peared before him, he threw his arms around his father and wept for a long time.

Israel said to Joseph, "Now I am ready to die, since I have seen for myself that you are still alive."

Then Joseph said to his brothers and to his father's household, "I will go up and speak to Pharaoh and will say to him, 'My brothers and my father's household, who were living in the land of Canaan, have come to me. The men are shepherds; they tend livestock, and they have brought along their flocks and herds and everything they own.' When Pharaoh calls you in and asks, 'What is your occupation?' you should answer, 'Your servants have tended livestock from our boyhood on, just as our fathers did.' Then you will be allowed to settle in the region of Goshen, for all shepherds are detestable to the Egyptians."

Jacob and his family set out for Egypt, but Jacob, being a changed man, makes time to build an altar and worship God for his blessings. Jacob makes sacrifices in thanksgiving. God then appears to Jacob again and confirms that he is to go down into Egypt and that he will bless him there and make them into a great nation. God even confirms that Joseph is alive and will be with Jacob when he dies.

With all their possessions, the entire family travels to Egypt and has an overwhelming reunion with Joseph, who provides the best land in Egypt for their flocks and his people to stay.

One of the major themes which have run through our studies of the patriarchs has been the message not to go down into Egypt. Now, this changes and Jacob is told to go down into Egypt.

This clearly shows to us that there is no place in the world where we may not go as long as it is in the will of God. Sometimes, we grow up being told we cannot go to certain places as they are bad places. In general, that may well be true, but God can use or visit those places too.

It is also important to note that although Egypt was a Godless place, God would still use Egypt for his purposes. Jacob's family would go down into Egypt and settle, and eventually, amid hardship and trial, become a formidable force.

Does that not often happen in the Church too? Is it not repeatedly in the midst of great trials that we have seen the most incredible growth in the Church? If it is God's will, the message to us is that we should not fear going into the world or facing trials. These will make us stronger if God is with us.

CHAPTER 22

Jacob's Death

Genesis 47:27-31, 49:29-33b
Now the Israelites settled in Egypt in the region of Goshen. They acquired property there and were fruitful and increased greatly in number.

Jacob lived in Egypt seventeen years, and the years of his life were a hundred and forty-seven. When the time drew near for Israel to die, he called for his son Joseph and said to him, "If I have found favor in your eyes, put your hand under my thigh and promise that you will show me kindness and faithfulness. Do not bury me in Egypt, but when I rest with my fathers, carry me out of Egypt and bury me where they are buried."

"I will do as you say," he said.

"Swear to me," he said. Then Joseph swore to him, and Israel worshiped as he leaned on the top of his staff.

Then he gave them these instructions: "I am about to be gathered to my people. Bury me with my fathers in the cave in the field of Ephron the Hittite, the cave in the field of Machpelah, near Mamre in Canaan, which Abraham bought along with the field as a burial place from Ephron the Hittite. There Abraham and his wife Sarah were buried, there Isaac and his wife Rebekah were buried, and there I buried Leah. The field and the cave in it were bought from the Hittites."

When Jacob had finished giving instructions to his sons, he drew his feet up into the bed, breathed his last and was gathered to his people.

Jacob was one hundred and thirty years old when he moved to Egypt, but he lived there for a further seventeen years and began to see his family grow into a nation and prosper.

At the end of the seventeen years, Jacob is aware that his time is up and is determined that he will not be buried in Egypt. Instead, he makes Joseph swear that he will carry him to Canaan and bury him in the cave where all his family was buried.

As soon as Jacob gets the reassurance and promise from Joseph, he is satisfied and gives up on life. He has had a long and rewarding life, despite his shaky beginnings, and is now ready to depart, knowing this is not the end.

When we come towards the end of our lives, to what will we look back? Will we look back and be happy that we have done all that God has asked us, or will we look back with regret that there are hundreds more we could have reached for God?

Many out there are lost and need a saviour, but it is not necessarily our job to reach them all. However, it is our job to answer the call of God in our lives, and failure to do this will leave bitter regrets as we near the end of our time.

Faith is a huge issue with the patriarchs, and it is still the same today. Is a lack of faith stopping us from stepping out into God's work today? As we near the end of our time, it is imperative to hold onto our faith. Just because we are old, it does not mean that God is done with us. As long as we are on this earth, God has work for us.

When the end comes, it is equally essential to maintain our faith. Jacob fully believed in God and knew that the future of his family was not in Egypt. He requested his body to be taken back and buried in the family grave in the promised land, confident that this is where the future lay for his people.

Author's Note

This marks the end of the book. If you have enjoyed this book, we would ask you to help us.

1. We would be grateful if you could leave a review of the book on Amazon. These reviews are the lifeblood of my business, and without them, I would have no new customers, and I could no longer write books.
2. I would welcome you to contact us through my author website at www.jamesgwhitelaw.com. I can assure you I am a real person and do not use a pen name. I will answer any questions you have as soon as I am able.
3. Finally, let your friends know that you read my book and enjoyed it on your social media pages.

Thank you for reading the book.

Scripture quotations taken from The Holy Bible, New International Version® NIV®

Copyright © 1973 1978 1984 2011 by Biblica, Inc. ™

Used by permission. All rights reserved worldwide.

www.ingramcontent.com/pod-product-compliance
Lightning Source LLC
Chambersburg PA
CBHW021448080526
44588CB00009B/751